The Economy

Can We Avert Disaster?

John Charles Daly, moderator

Arthur F. Burns
Robert N. Giaimo
William Proxmire
Henry S. Reuss

Held on April 1, 1980
and sponsored by
the American Enterprise Institute
for Public Policy Research
Washington, D.C.

This pamphlet contains the edited transcript
of one of a series of AEI forums.
These forums offer a medium for
informal exchanges of ideas on current policy problems
of national and international import.
As part of AEI's program of providing opportunities
for the presentation of competing views,
they serve to enhance the prospect
that decisions within our democracy will be based
on a more informed public opinion.
AEI forums are also available on
audio and color-video cassettes.

AEI Forum 39

ISBN 0-8447-2182-4
Library of Congress Catalog Card No. 80–66297
Printed in the United States of America

JOHN CHARLES DALY, former ABC News chief and forum moderator: This public policy forum, part of a series presented by the American Enterprise Institute, is concerned, to be blunt, with our daily bread and butter. Our subject, "The Economy: Can We Avert Disaster?"

The speculative fever in the marketplace is matched by fevered speculation as to what is going on and what to do about it. Looming over all is the dread memory of the past: the Great Depression of the 1930s. Inflation is raging, productivity is declining, interest rates are at stunning levels, and the National Savings Pool for Investment is massively invaded by federal credit programs when private sector investment is desperately needed to restore vitality and efficiency in the economy. The economy is a labyrinth of goods and services, wages and prices, credit and debt, budgets and projections, fiscal and monetary policies, inflation rates and interest rates, taxes and tax cuts, and theories and facts.

Dr. Burns, what would you prescribe for our economic malaise?

ARTHUR F. BURNS, former chairman of the board of governors, Federal Reserve System: You have described our economic condition quite accurately. The critical problem facing our country now is to turn inflationary psychology around. The Congress, and also the White House, seem simply to be concerned with minor, marginal adjustments. To turn inflationary psychology around, we need to give people confidence that the long era of persistent budget deficits will come to an end. We need to make it much more difficult, therefore, to run budget deficits in the future.

Second, we need structural adjustments. The Congress, in fact, during the past few years has legislated inflation through its agricultural policies and through its wage policies.

Next, the Federal Reserve must have the strong support of the Congress in pursuing a restrictive monetary policy.

Finally, Congress should pass legislation now scheduling a tax reduction for each of the next five to seven years, the reduction to be merely symbolic, minor, in the first two years, because we cannot afford to enlarge our deficit and to nourish inflation any further. The tax reduction should be substantial in later years and be of a kind that will improve the nation's productivity, that will enable us to rebuild our obsolete industrial plant. That will be very helpful to our country's future.

MR. DALY: Representative Giaimo, as chairman of the House Budget Committee, what is your opinion?

ROBERT N. GIAIMO, U.S. representative (Democrat, Connecticut): We in Congress must play our part in bringing inflation under control. The American people must cooperate. We must change our way of living. We must live within our means more than we have, if we hope to bring inflation under control.

We in Congress can do some specific things, and we are beginning to do them. I predict that the House and the Senate will make substantial cuts for the first time in the 1981 budget, cuts totaling somewhere around $21 billion or $22 billion, which are real reductions in spending. I predict that the House and the Senate will also provide for tax cuts designed specifically to increase productivity, which is what we must do to control inflation.

This is a great change for Congress. It says to the states and to the communities that they must reduce their dependence on Washington for assistance. That is a good change and it will help to reduce inflation.

MR. DALY: Senator Proxmire, as chairman of the Senate Banking, Housing, and Urban Affairs Committee and as a member of the Senate Appropriations Committee and of the Joint Economic Committee, what is your prescription?

WILLIAM PROXMIRE, U.S. senator (Democrat, Wisconsin): I agree with both Bob Giaimo and Arthur Burns. We must have a much, much deeper cut than the President has requested or than the Congress, so far, has indicated it favors; we need a cut of something like $30 billion. Furthermore we must make sure that that kind of reduction is continued in 1982, 1983, and throughout this decade. One year of a balanced budget will not do it. Persistence will be difficult, because we may very well be faced with a recession this year.

I hope that under those circumstances, we will continue to hold down spending. And I hope that if we do take action to counteract the inflation, we do it with tax deductions. That is difficult to do, but I hope we do that.

I hope that we get under contol the federal credit programs, which have gotten out of line. They have proliferated even more than the budget has. We were increasing those federal credit programs at a more rapid rate than the deficit was increasing. For instance, it was a serious mistake to bail out Chrysler, to bail out New York City.

Finally, we must do something to encourage people to save money. That is the same sort of thing Bob Giaimo was saying when he indicated people must live within their means. Our savings rate is a disgrace now. It is lower than it has been at any time since we started keeping statistics. It is lower than that of any other developed country. We must encourage people to save money by getting a grip on inflation and by providing the kind of tax incentives that would persuade people that it makes sense to save their money.

MR. DALY: Representative Reuss is chairman of the House Banking, Finance and Urban Affairs Committee and also a member of the Joint Economic Committee. What course would you set for our economy?

HENRY S. REUSS, U.S. representative (Democrat, Wisconsin): At the center of our fight against inflation, I would erect on the top of the hill a mighty fortress called structural reform. Our economy has become ramshackle, and we need to modernize it, to reindustrialize America, to get productivity going. I think it is disgraceful that we are letting our steel industry go to rack and ruin; our automobiles are made in Germany and Japan. Our semiconductor industry, our color television industry, our mass transit vehicle industry, not to mention the textile industry, the shoe industry, and so many other industries, are leaving America. This is madness. We must reindustrialize.

Surrounding this central fortress of structural reform, I would erect four outworks, four subfortifications: a balanced budget; a monetary policy of restraint; a significant reduction in our dependence on oil from the member nations of the Organization of Petroleum Exporting Countries (OPEC); and, with those things in place, I would advocate a price-wage freeze for six months. After the six months, with these structural reforms in place, we could afford to remove the freeze and adopt a social contract between management, labor, and government that might stick, as it has in countries like Germany and Austria.

MR. DALY: You have all indicated the major elements in the economy that need action. Let's begin with one of the principal ones.

Dr. Burns urgently called for an end to budget deficits. Will the proposed administration and/or congressional budget cuts for Fiscal Years 1980 and 1981—the year in which we hope for the balanced budget—be decisive in stabilizing the economy?

DR. BURNS: I was glad to hear members of the Congress speak of larger budgetary revisions than have, as yet, been advocated by the

White House. The White House has developed a habit, recently, of changing its mind about the budget at rather short intervals. I don't know where it will stand tomorrow. But as things stand now, after all the revisions that the President has gone through, outlays for this fiscal year will go up by $5.4 billion if the President's recommendations are followed. They will come down next fiscal year by something like $4 billion. Therefore, I see much ado about next to nothing.

We must do a great deal better than that. I was very pleased to hear Senator Proxmire's pronouncement on what is needed along budgetary lines.

REPRESENTATIVE GIAIMO: The administration's cuts bring outlays for Fiscal Year 1981 to around $612 billion. That is a reduction from about $628 billion. That represents a substantial reduction in programs. In addition to that, the administration has a legislative reform package—which Congress traditionally ignores and which we hope it will not ignore this year—that includes about $5 billion in legislative reforms, affecting hospital cost containment, impact aid, veterans programs, school lunch programs, and many others.

We must also consider that $5 billion recommended as a reduction. If the reduction does not take place, that money will have to be added back to the budget in the fall, as it will have to be added back to the 1980 budget, because we have done little in 1980 by way of legislative reforms. So there are substantial cuts.

SENATOR PROXMIRE: The reestimation that you mentioned means that because of inflation, which was unanticipated, and because of much higher interest costs for the federal government, the expenditures are going up from the estimated $616 billion to about $627 billion.

REPRESENTATIVE GIAIMO: Correct.

SENATOR PROXMIRE: Even so, I agree with Dr. Burns's point that that is all the more reason why we need a deeper cut. I know it is very hard. You, personally, have done more than anybody else I know of; you have been at every one of those sessions with the administration trying to cut the budget, and it is extremely hard to do it.

An example of what we must do: Instead of just cutting the states' share of revenue sharing, we must cut out all revenue sharing. I realize the effect on the localities makes this very difficult, but that is something we have to do. I think we have to cut military spending, because there is waste and fat there just as there is everywhere else.

The President has proposed very limited reductions in military spending mainly by not replacing quite so rapidly people who leave the service. It seems to me we can cut $5 billion or $6 billion there. I have specified some of the cuts I would make; others have other areas. These cuts would give us a stronger, leaner, meaner military operation.

Congress must take its share of the cuts. We must cut our staffs, as an example. If we spread these reductions across the government, which is very difficult to do, we can make a $30 billion or $35 billion reduction.

DR. BURNS: What this country needs is a sense of stability; otherwise we will not reestablish confidence in our country's future. The last thing I want to do is to get into an arithmetical debate; that would only cause confusion. But let me remind you that in January of this year, when the President presented his outlay estimate—a figure that was $37 billion larger than his original estimate for this fiscal year—the figure was $16 billion more than the official estimate as of three months earlier; that on March 14, when the President revised his budget estimate, the net effect was to increase by $4 billion the outlays for this fiscal year. When he revised his budget once again the other day, it was $1.3 billion more than it was on March 14. This is very troublesome and very confusing to our country. We need some stability.

Let the Congress decide on a level of expenditure and make a determined effort to stay with it.

SENATOR PROXMIRE: In all fairness, is it not true, though, that nobody really anticipated the colossal increase in interest rates, nobody anticipated the tremendous increase in inflation, and that an estimate made from the perspective of March must reflect what has happened to interest rates, what has happened to inflation? That represents an increase of about $10 billion or $15 billion.

DR. BURNS: It is true, but you must not overlook the fact that the rapid increase in government spending and the enormous budget deficits that we have been running year after year are, in large part, responsible for the very inflation of which you speak.

REPRESENTATIVE REUSS: I congratulate my colleagues, Representative Giaimo and Senator Proxmire. They are tigers on the budget, and I am happy we have them. I favor a balanced budget, too.

I would put in one qualification on that balanced budget. To the maximum possible extent, we must preserve, in our austere balanced budget, the programs that provide jobs for people who live in poverty pockets, because they are the people who are hurt by budgetary austerity. We must reduce social tension. The most perfect economics in the world will not save us if we break out in civil strife. We can have a balanced budget and still do our best for those who need jobs.

SENATOR PROXMIRE: On that subject, I talked today to AFL–CIO representatives from Wisconsin, including people from Milwaukee, and they tell me that the Comprehensive Employment and Training Act (CETA) is worth nothing if the private sector does not move ahead. The private sector now is plagued by high interest rates, as far as construction and home building are concerned, and it cannot provide jobs for people who come out of CETA with training because inflationary policies make it impossible for the private sector to do the kind of job it ought to do.

REPRESENTATIVE REUSS: I completely agree. CETA is no favorite of mine. Too often it simply involves a city government rehiring some junior planner it fired last week. That does not make contact with the problem at all. I am talking about private sector jobs. I am talking about expanding the very sensible beginning of a program we have, which subsidizes private employment. I agree with Arthur Burns that a differential minimum wage might do some good. We could at least try it in several areas. We simply must do something about the 50 percent unemployment in the ghetto; we must do something about the pockets of rural poverty.

REPRESENTATIVE GIAIMO: Let me set the record straight that we have not done away with CETA. We have cut CETA, we have cut it substantially; so has the President. But there is a substantial portion left. There will be job programs, and in some of these related, allied areas.

You raise a good question when you speak of the minimum wage and the youth differential. We must look at the whole problem of indexation in our country, which no one is addressing as yet.

As you know, Senator Proxmire, when we had meetings with the leadership of the House and Senate and senior members of the administration to discuss these issues, there was a general consensus that we could not tamper with the cost-of-living index adjustments which, in many instances, overstated inflation. I think we must address that.

I certainly agree that we ought to experiment with a youth differential in minimum wage. But until we begin to tackle those problems, it will be hard to get the federal government out of the business of sustaining these programs and these communities and these projects.

REPRESENTATIVE REUSS: Let's do both at the same time.

DR. BURNS: May I say this, particularly to my congressional friends? As a professional educator for many years, I have favored programs of training and retraining. I have watched them grow, and they have multiplied. And I look for the effects. I find that youth unemployment, where supposedly much of the money has been spent, has declined less than unemployment of adults, men or women. This is something that calls for a congressional inquiry. We are spending many billions of dollars for training and retraining. What benefits are we deriving from it? Where is the money going? How many carpenters are we training? Things may have changed in the last two or three years, but when I looked into the matter last, I could get all kinds of statistics on manpower training programs by bureaucratic categories, but I could not find out how many carpenters, or how many steam fitters, or how many plumbers were being trained. I think Congress ought to hold hearings on this subject.

REPRESENTATIVE REUSS: We certainly ought to, Dr. Burns; you are on the right track. The District of Columbia is now in the throes of a tremendous boom of what some call paragovernmental activities: the multinationals, the think tanks, the service industries are spawning new jobs at a great rate, yet the educational system—primary, secondary, and college—of the District of Columbia is not geared to it. We ought to look at that. We ought to prepare people for the jobs that will exist three years from now, five years from now.

SENATOR PROXMIRE: Let me get back, very quickly, to a very interesting point Representative Giaimo made about how indexing social security, for example, results in a situation in which we overstate the inflation because of the emphasis, particularly in housing. It assumes that everybody buys one twelfth of a house a year. We know that most of the people on social security do not do anything like that. Mortgage interest rates and housing prices have increased enormously. To indicate how complicated this whole business is, if we should now shift, what would happen is that we would probably, once again, overcompensate. What will happen, in my view, over the next few months, is that housing prices will level off. They will begin to drop. Interest rates, I think, will begin to go down. The housing component will be one area of the economy that will hold down the consumer price index (CPI) and, therefore, hold down the payments under social security.

So, if we start shifting the summary on the statistics at this time, we will accomplish exactly the opposite of what you want to do—we will be spending more, not less.

REPRESENTATIVE GIAIMO: You run that risk, but in addition to simply correcting the CPI formula, we should look at the issue of indexation in principle to determine whether or not it is correct to index fully for inflation. I do not think it is.

SENATOR PROXMIRE: It institutionalizes inflation. There is no way inflation can be stopped that way.

REPRESENTATIVE GIAIMO: I do not think cost-of-living adjustments should totally compensate for inflation. I think they should be somewhat less.

DR. BURNS: I have worked in this area for many years, and I have very grave doubts about the kind of debating that is going on.

What the White House or, if not the White House, the Congress ought to do is to appoint a technical commission and let it report back in three to six months on the present cost-of-living index or the consumer price index and recommend what revisions might best be made in the interest of accuracy.

There is another approach to the indexation problem. Take social security, for example. I think I would count one half of social security benefits as part of an individual's income and let him then be taxed according to the tax tables. In that way, the very poorest people would be protected. And the tax payments of those who receive middle incomes or high incomes would go up. That would reduce the burden that social security now places on our budget and, at the same time, protect the poor people.

Congress made a start in that direction in connection with unemployment insurance.

SENATOR PROXMIRE: I just wonder how really productive that kind of tax could be, because the people in the higher part of social security still have low incomes. It is my understanding that the average social security recipient receives $6,000 a year. The average couple, not much more than that—$7,000 a year. These days, that is very close to a poverty wage. It is true that the income tax would be relatively light as a percentage of their income, but it would still be painful for them. And I do not think it would yield a great deal because of the very low incomes that most of the people on social security have.

DR. BURNS: If you don't like my approach, you can adjust it, the way you did in connection with unemployment insurance, where you now tax the unemployment insurance benefits that an individual receives when his overall income, including unemployment benefits, is $20,000 or over.

SENATOR PROXMIRE: I agree with that. I see no reason why we should not tax unemployment compensation.

DR. BURNS: Some principle along those lines could be worked out.

REPRESENTATIVE GIAIMO: You know, Dr. Burns, I am retiring from Congress this year. I am not running for reelection.

DR. BURNS: I am sorry to see you retire at this stage when you have become the budget cutter.

REPRESENTATIVE GIAIMO: Thank you. So I can say that there is some merit. We certainly ought at least to look into the issue of taxation of social security, as the commission recommended. But as a practical matter, as you know, even to suggest that in the Congress is politically unwise.

DR. BURNS: Let me ask you a political question. Would taxing social security benefits, as far as the upper income groups are concerned, be more acceptable or less acceptable than indexation, or reduced indexation, which is what you propose?

REPRESENTATIVE GIAIMO: It would be less acceptable.

MR. DALY: For our audience, will one of you take on the job of defining indexation? Some may not be familiar with that term.

REPRESENTATIVE GIAIMO: Indexation, as I understand it, is an automatic cost-of-living adjustment each year, based on the inflation rate, for social security recipients and for veterans who receive compensation or pensions. In other words, we compensate for inflation. And we do that also with retirees from the federal government.

MR. DALY: Are you discussing this as indexing across the board?

SENATOR PROXMIRE: We already index wages as a matter of collective bargaining. But the point that Representative Giaimo made earlier relates to that. I do not know of any case in which wages are fully indexed. For instance, most of the United Auto Workers (UAW) employees get a partial reimbursement on inflation, but only partial; they do not get full compensation unless they make less than $6.50 or $7.00 an hour.

DR. BURNS: Overall, they do not do too badly.

SENATOR PROXMIRE: That's right, but it has an inflationary effect.

REPRESENTATIVE GIAIMO: As you know, we do not index fully for military and civilian employees. The President has put a ceiling on that, in recent years at 7 percent or 7½ percent. It is something less than the total inflation rate.

REPRESENTATIVE REUSS: Before you leave indexation, I want to register one gripe. Very highly paid civil servants who are retired and—I blush—congressmen and senators who are retired get a nice cost-of-living index on their whole $35,000, or whatever it is they get a year. That is not right. They should be indexed on what you might call the market basket, which reflects their food, their clothing, and their rents—say, the first $20,000.

Beyond that, indexation is an attempt to allow everybody in America to keep his particular share. The rich get richer, and so on. It is really quite nutty, and we ought to take a look at that.

You could be a great hero, Bob, and twice a year. [Laughter.]

MR. DALY: Senator Proxmire, you raised a basic truth. There are, in reality, two federal budgets: the expenditure budget, about which we hear a great deal, and the credit budget, about which there is very little publicity or understanding.

DR. BURNS: You are going to raise a question about the revenue side of the budget as well, I hope?

MR. DALY: Yes, I hope we can get to it. Would you define the credit budget, what it incorporates, and its scope within the economy?

SENATOR PROXMIRE: The credit budget, of course, consists of federal credit programs in which the federal government either borrows or guarantees borrowing. Much of it is outside the budget. The federal government has a device called the Federal Financing Bank, which completely avoids the appropriation process and is outside the budget. For some reason, some agencies are able to borrow from the Federal Financing Bank. Whenever a program may cause real distress in the budget because of the size of the outlay, someone suggests that it be put in the Federal Financing Bank. If the program acquires enough clout, it will be put in the Federal Financing Bank as a way of avoiding the budget.

In general, your question relating to federal credit programs falls into the area of interest of both Henry Reuss and myself, because our banking committees oversee the federal credit programs. Some of the programs are in the budget, some are not. These federal credit programs have been expanding very rapidly, and they cover guarantees. A guarantee does not require the government to make a loan, so the program need not be traced through the budget. A guarantee provides risk-free credit to a particular entity—Chrysler Corporation, New York City, whatever. That entity will be able to get credit. Other people, of course, do not have that kind of guarantee, so they, in effect, lose credit. The fact that Chrysler, for example, got a $1.5 billion guarantee means that there are 15,000 farmers or small businessmen who could each have gotten a $100,000 loan in place of Chrysler.

MR. DALY: How large is this credit budget?

SENATOR PROXMIRE: Altogether it will be larger in 1981 than the regular federal budget. It amounts to more than $600 billion. Am I right, Dr. Burns? $670 billion, something in that area?

DR. BURNS: I don't remember the amount of the outstanding loans, but the addition to the outstanding loans is around $57 billion for Fiscal Year 1981.

SENATOR PROXMIRE: Yes.

MR. DALY: Do you think that this should be brought under control, and if so, how?

SENATOR PROXMIRE: Yes. I have written to the Budget Committee and argued that we ought to have a regular process with the same kind of budgetary disciplines that we have in the appropriation process. Guarantees could be brought in in tandem with the regular budget, on which we set a limit, and on which we have to argue painfully in determining priorities. It seems to me this would help hold down the guarantees we give so broadly and so easily. It means we would have to balance one against another, and it means there would then be less of a burden on the private capital market. That would tend to hold interest rates down.

MR. DALY: Dr. Burns, you wanted to discuss the revenue budget?

DR. BURNS: Yes. I must say that I am very much disturbed by the revised budget message that the White House has sent to the Congress. The revised budget message calls for an increase in revenues in this fiscal year of $8 billion, as against the lower figure that was presented in January. It calls for an increase in tax revenues for Fiscal Year 1981 of $28 billion, another increase over the figure presented just two months ago.

As things now stand, in January the President called for an increase for Fiscal Year 1981 of $76 billion. He has added $28 billion to that. If these figures are realized in practice—they are estimates, recommendations, at the present time—tax revenues will go up by more than $100 billion next year. We will find that the average tax rate in this country, or tax revenues expressed as a percentage of the gross national product, will be more than 22 percent and will be higher than in any year, I believe, in our nation's history, higher than in the peak war year of 1944.

SENATOR PROXMIRE: Isn't a great deal of this because of inflation? On part of it, you're undoubtedly correct. Part of it certainly is the calculated effort to increase the gasoline tax by $10 billion and also to withhold dividends and interest, which, in a way, is increasing taxes. But almost all the rest of it is because we now have recalculated our inflation, and, of course, that will have an effect on federal revenues, because nominal incomes will be higher. Isn't that a large part of the explanation?

DR. BURNS: I agree with that, but that doesn't tell you or me or our country what will be the effect on the economy of such an enormous increase in tax revenues.

REPRESENTATIVE GIAIMO: That's why it's essential. I think the heavy increase in revenues over the President's original estimates, which were a combination of inflation plus what Senator Proxmire mentioned, indicates that inflation is wreaking havoc with our economic projections and with our ability to keep our economy sound. The most important thing we can do, therefore, is to try to get the inflation rate down. That means many things, one of which we in Congress can do, and that is to reduce spending. So we are reducing on the spending side of the budget.

At the same time, I don't think we would want a type of tax reduction that would be inflationary in this period and would contravene what we are trying to do.

MR. DALY: Let's move on to a broader pattern in this area. You mentioned price controls. There is an expanding demand for wage and price controls. Do you think that mandatory wage and price controls can lower the inflation rate markedly and hold it for the long term, or do you think it would be short-term and dangerous?

REPRESENTATIVE REUSS: If all we did was apply price-wage controls to the present ramshackled, unproductive, rickety economy, it would be worse than useless; it would be a disaster, because we would simply freeze in place all the rigidities that everybody, including Congress, has built into the system.

If, however, we attack what I regard as the central problem, structural reform, we can balance the budget. We should balance the budget until we are blue in the face. We can tighten money until the pips squeak, but unless we do something about the structure of our economy, we will not really come to grips with inflation.

It would have been a great thing if, three years ago, a government-business-labor team headed by, for example, a Father Theodore Hesburgh, had gone to Detroit and observed that OPEC was raising the price of gasoline terribly and that Detroit was still making gas guzzlers while Volkswagen and the Japanese manufacturers were making gas-conserving cars. If we had found out what Detroit needed—capital, regulation, labor, whatever—I don't think we'd be in the terrible pickle we're in now. The same applies to steel and dozens of other industries.

I would support price controls, but only as a temporary measure, incident to a thoroughgoing reform. But since we aren't embarking on that thoroughgoing reform, I am not, in the present situation, for price controls.

SENATOR PROXMIRE: But the problem is not that wage-price controls or wage-price freezes undermine the constituency that is, at last, pushing the Congress to do the things it should.

Why do we have this constituency? Why do we, for the first time, have members of Congress—and I think it's a substantial majority in both parties—anxious to hold down spending and balance the budget? It is because people are so concerned about inflation; they taste it, they see it. A wage-price freeze that makes inflation seem to be under control will cause the same problem we had in 1971–1973, which was a disaster. It began with inflation at 4 percent. We instituted a wage-price freeze. It lasted a few months. It worked fairly well. Then prices began to climb. By the time we took off the freeze, the inflation rate was 10 percent.

REPRESENTATIVE REUSS: And I'll tell you why. That was under Mr. Nixon's administration. He so perforated the economy with import taxes and export controls and other things that made the economic structure worse that, of course, when price controls were removed, there was an explosion.

I don't think it would really weaken the constituency. I am with you for a balanced budget. I am with Arthur Burns for a control over the monetary supply. But we need all these things in harmony; then they make sense.

DR. BURNS: If I understand you, Representative Reuss, you would not want to go to mandatory controls until some fundamental structural reforms were under way.

REPRESENTATIVE REUSS: Absolutely.

DR. BURNS: And since they are not, as yet, underway, do I understand you to say that you, at the present time, are opposed to mandatory controls?

REPRESENTATIVE REUSS: You've expressed my position better than I did.

DR. BURNS: Thank you very much. I am not willing even to talk about controls until some fundamental reforms are underway. Then I might be willing to talk about them.

REPRESENTATIVE REUSS: I know the danger of talking about them, because it is said that in anticipation business raises its prices, labor raises its wages. There's something to be said for that. When I do talk about it, I make clear that I am opposed to controls now, and they won't happen because Senator Proxmire and I are the banking chairmen, and they have to come through us. I testified the other day against them. But that doesn't mean that later on they might not have an appropriate place.

DR. BURNS: I think that's good news for the country.

MR. DALY: This is a very sophisticated area, Dr. Burns, and I'm not quite sure that those of us in the audience who are not economists will ever really understand it. Monetary policy, we hear and read, is critically important to a stable economy. What are we doing that we should not do and what should we do that we are not doing?

DR. BURNS: By and large, the Federal Reserve is on the right track. It has been seeking to restrain the growth of money and credit. And I believe it is beginning to get some results.

At the same time, I am very sorry to add that the invocation by the President of the Credit Control Act of 1969 is most unfortunate. The Federal Reserve has now gone in for credit allocations of all sorts. That act ought to be repealed by the Congress, and the sooner the better. Under that act, the Federal Reserve Board has virtually dictatorial power over our economy. No agency of government should have that power.

REPRESENTATIVE REUSS: I agree with Arthur Burns that some of the actions taken under the Credit Control Act by the Federal Reserve seem ill-advised.

But let's take the subject of credit allocation, which is a longstanding bone of contention between my friend Dr. Burns and myself. I believe it would be a good thing for the country if the Federal Reserve consistently maintained as tight an overall control over the money supply as you and I would want and if it asked the major banks in the country to report every month on the percentage of loans made in the inflationary area, loans for speculation in silver, gold, land, and commodities, loans for corporate takeovers that are just for the sake of aggrandizement, and the percentage of loans that fight inflation, loans for home building, which will sop up purchasing power, loans for capital equipment, which will increase productivity and fight inflation.

The public could then be entrusted with looking at these monthly figures, and bankers would then have a reasonable excuse to turn down speculative borrowers. That would bring down the interest rate on housing and on capital investment, which is where we need to bring it down.

SENATOR PROXMIRE: Monetary policy to most Americans means interest rates. That's the way they see it. The cruelest effect of the inflation now is high interest rates and their effect on home builders and so forth.

We must make people understand that there is no way to lower the interest rate below the inflation rate. If it were legislated lower, it would create a field day for speculators. They would borrow money at the lower rate of interest and put it into almost anything: commodities, land, whatever. Then they would be able to pay back, of course, at a lower level and to make money out of the banker's or the lender's funds. That will aggravate inflation by encouraging speculation. That's why the interest rate has to be high. None of us likes it. I don't know a banker who likes it. Certainly, the people here in Washington recognize its terrible effect on farmers, small businessmen, and home builders. But, unfortunately, that's the price we have to pay for inflation.

DR. BURNS: Senator Proxmire has put the matter very well, indeed. I would only add that one basic reason why interest rates are so high at the present time is that the Federal Reserve has been carrying almost the entire burden of fighting inflation. Now it is up to the White House and it is up to the Congress to lighten the burden that has been imposed on the Federal Reserve.

MR. DALY: Let me ask a final question: Are we going to have a recession? When will it come? How long will it last? And how deep will it be?

SENATOR PROXMIRE: These things cannot be predicted. The economists predicted a recession all through 1979; they were consistently wrong. I feel that a drop in housing starts such as we have is likely to lead to a recession. My expectation is that we will have a serious recession, unfortunately, this year.

DR. BURNS: We are moving into a recession, definitely. How serious it will be, I have no way of knowing.

REPRESENTATIVE GIAIMO: There is a recession out there, but the major problem we have to concern ourselves with right now is this inflation and trying to bring it down. When the recession hits, then we'll have to study that problem and do our best. But right now, the problem is inflation, and nothing else.

MR. DALY: Representative Reuss?

REPRESENTATIVE REUSS: On predictions, as far as I'm concerned, silence is golden. [Laughter.]

MR. DALY: We have put down a very broad base. Now we can have a dialogue with our guests in the audience.

GOTTFRIED HABERLER, American Enterprise Institute: The panelists agree that inflation has to be brought down and that we need tight money and a balanced budget. Is it possible to avoid a recession if we do that? Structural reforms, of course, may help, but they come only much later. Is it possible to avoid a recession if we want to bring the inflation down?

DR. BURNS: Even if we had not had the new budgetary messages and the new enthusiasm—I hope it lasts—in the Congress to keep the budget down, a recession would have developed in the country. And the new policy, particularly the strong credit restraints that are being applied by the Federal Reserve at the present time, will hasten the onset of a recession and perhaps also intensify it.

SENATOR PROXMIRE: We have to understand that a recession is as much a part of the free enterprise system as expansion. A free enterprise system cannot always be in an expansionary period. The key is to have a recession that we hope is not deep and not long and is not as painful as it might be. But there is just no way to get prices down without a decline in the nominal GNP. In fact, Dr. Burns and the other members of the panel are probably much more familiar with economic history than I am, but I doubt there have been many times in history when inflation dropped while the nominal GNP was rising. That is a tough price we have to pay, but it is a price that somehow will have to be paid.

REPRESENTATIVE GIAIMO: It is important to remember that our monetary policy, as enunciated by the Federal Reserve for some time, and our fiscal policy, as demonstrated by slowing down on the rate of growth in our economy, are designed to slow down the economy.

That, to a degree, means less growth and, therefore, some form of recession or slowdown.

Recession is just another word for slowdown, and our policies are designed to bring that about. This is what is historically called austerity, and it is one of the proven methods of slowing down inflation. It's cruel and it hurts, but it has to be done.

REPRESENTATIVE REUSS: I disagree with my colleague. I think, Dr. Haberler, that it is possible to have monetary restraint and fiscal restraint and avoid a recession. By recession I mean at least six months when growth becomes negative, when productivity declines. I think we can do that if we make our budget restraint save the sensible programs that make jobs and if we make our monetary restraints save capital investments at the expense of speculation. It can be done. We do not have to have 20 percent interest rates. If that doesn't work, then we have 25 percent interest rates. It's like the barber surgeons of the Middle Ages: if bleeding you didn't cure you, they would bleed you some more.

I don't think it is necessary. I think by adopting some human attributes in these programs, we can avoid a recession.

SENATOR PROXMIRE: Forever? No recession ever?

REPRESENTATIVE REUSS: No, not forever. I wouldn't say forever.

SENATOR PROXMIRE: Then what are we talking about?

REPRESENTATIVE REUSS: I am talking about how we can get out of our inflation now. I believe we can get out of our inflation without incurring a recession. Sure, we have to slow growth, absolutely; but I don't see why we have to go into negative.

DR. HABERLER: Which means you have abolished the business cycle. You don't need a recession.

REPRESENTATIVE REUSS: No. I would abolish the boom-bust. I am against extreme, speculative booms, and I am against busts. Why don't we slow down the growth? Why do we have to have millions of additional unemployed?

SENATOR PROXMIRE: That reminds me of the old southern senator who said I am against inflation; I'm against deflation; I'm for flation. [Laughter.]

REPRESENTATIVE REUSS: The old southern senator Stephen Leacock.

HERMAN SMITH, National Association of Home Builders: We have heard home building and home buyers mentioned earlier tonight. As this industry faces a decline in excess of 50 percent, and as we are facing the fact that only about 4 percent of American families can now qualify for a medium-price home, rather than destroy an industry, what do we see in the near future for some temporary relief to the home buyer and the 1.6 million employees who will be laid off within the next year in this industry?

REPRESENTATIVE REUSS: In terms of short-term relief, there is some activity by the Federal Home Loan Bank Board to make more money available to the thrift institutions. That is a little thing, but something.

Congress is considering a revival of the Brooke-Cranston Act which, if properly constructed, can help. Almost every other industrialized democracy in the world tempers its tight money policy to the shorn lamb of the housing industry. In one form or another, within the parameters of tight money, less money goes to speculation and to takeovers and more to home building and other forms of capital investment. We need all of those things.

SENATOR PROXMIRE: I'm very impressed by your group, Mr. Smith. They came to see me, and they indicated that they believe that the only way really to solve their problem is to get inflation under control. They were much more strongly for reducing federal spending than for any other approach. They did say that they were interested in Brooke-Cranston, but they want a Brooke-Cranston that can be put into effect. If we enact that, we will have to find money elsewhere. We will have to make cuts in the budget to make it possible to provide additional funds for housing, which is very hard to do.

MR. DALY: Would you tell us about the Brooke-Cranston Act?

SENATOR PROXMIRE: The Brooke-Cranston Act provides a subsidy for housing programs by empowering the federal government to buy mortgages, in effect buying the homes that people cannot now sell. With $10 billion, they could buy $10 billion worth of mortgages. At $50,000 a mortgage, that's 200,000 housing starts. If it did nothing else, it would relieve the inventory.

But it would also, of course, increase production. It would increase employment in the housing industry. It is, however, a proposal that would have a fantastic effect on the budget if those mortgages were not sold promptly. There is no way it could be accepted.

There is one other proposal under consideration that wouldn't have such an effect on the budget. There is $185 million still available from the old 235 program, a homeownership program for low-income people. It was impounded by President Nixon, never spent; it is already authorized and, as I understand it, appropriated. The funds are there. If we altered the legislation to permit that money to be used for interest subsidies, we could get 100,000 housing starts out of that. But the program would have to be modified to make it possible to apply this to middle-income people. That's where housing sales would have to be, if the program were to be carried out on a big basis.

MR. DALY: Dr. Burns, what is wrong with going back to something that we did with at least some success earlier in our history, creating a quasi-public corporation like the Reconstruction Finance Corporation (RFC). The ten-cents-a-gallon tax that will yield $10 billion would be turned over to that RFC, which in turn would lend it to savings and loans at 5½ percent interest with a proviso that it must lend it out at no more than 7 percent interest on homes not to cost more than $50,000.

The public would earn money on its investment. The savings and loans, which are going against the wall because the money market funds are driving them up, would profit. And it would revive the housing industry. It could be responsible for creating 200,000 new homes, furniture, appliances, and so forth. Now, Dr. Burns, tell me it doesn't make any sense.

DR. BURNS: I think Brooke-Cranston would give a minor lift to home building. But the home building industry is headed for something under 1 million starts. Through various government-controlled grants, we could get an additional 30,000–100,000 starts. The industry would applaud it. But that's not a solution to the problem.

As long as market interest rates remain at their present level, the thrift institutions will lose funds. Their ability to lend on mortgages will be curtailed. As long as inflation continues, even if the thrift institutions have all the money, those who want to buy a home will not qualify as bankers look over the prospect of individuals' being able to service the debt.

There is only one way, really, to tackle the problem, and that is to create an environment in which inflationary psychology turns around, in which people expect that inflation will be curbed. Then the premium that is built into interest rates will come down and the housing industry can flourish once again. In the absence of that, I think we are just chasing a rainbow.

SENATOR PROXMIRE: Dr. Burns, that's beautiful, and I agree wholeheartedly with it. The difficulty, however, is that, as I understand Mr. Smith's question, he asked what could be done now. And is the answer nothing?

DR. BURNS: The answer is very little.

MR. SMITH: Home builders are twisting in the wind on a string right now.

SENATOR PROXMIRE: They certainly are dying. I have never seen an industry hit harder.

REPRESENTATIVE GIAIMO: Nevertheless, what can they do? We must bring interest rates down. How do we get interest rates down? By reducing inflation, which means reducing the rate of growth. There are many things we must do. One of them is to continue the tight money policy of the Federal Reserve. We in government must reduce our expenditure levels. There are a lot of other things that must be done, as Henry Reuss has indicated.

Some of you were talking about possible new programs. Part of the inflationary spiral we are in is the result of overregulation in many industries. We must slow down the whole process.

A basic problem that we are looking at but not recognizing is that we must increase productivity. That means creating a favorable climate for people to invest, reducing government expenditures, reducing government regulation.

I hate to sound as if this is something novel, but I think it is time that we begin to do this. Until we do, Americans will suffer, businesses will suffer. And the housing industry is suffering probably more than any.

SENATOR PROXMIRE: Almost all home builders are small businesses. They may sell fifty homes in a year.

Some of these fellows have interest payments of $40,000 a month now. It is killing them. They are dying. They sold fifty houses last year. This year they will sell four or five. They have to lay off all their employees. Very efficient, competent, conscientious people who have been in the business all their lives are getting out of it. They are driven out of it, and that is bad for the economy.

REPRESENTATIVE REUSS: We cannot just let the iron law of nature knock out the home building industry. To do that would add to inflation, because those home builders go broke. They disband their crews. Then when things pick up, they have to put together very hastily another crew, and of course, they charge higher prices because they don't know what they are doing. So we then have another round of inflation.

This stop-go pattern ruined the United Kingdom, and it will ruin the United States unless we pull up our suspenders rather fast.

ROBERT HILL, National Urban League Research Department: Most of you feel that we will probably have a recession, but it seems to me quite clear that we are really talking about balancing the budget by deliberately increasing already high levels of unemployment. We definitely are talking about increasing the level of unemployment. We say this may be cruel, but we also have to acknowledge that it will not be differentially shared by everyone. There is a pecking order with respect to unemployment. Many of those who were the last hired will be the first fired. The more we get into a recession, the more people may be unemployed. It does seem to me, however, that this balanced budget is something of a mirage, because we are deliberately increasing unemployment, and in the budget we are talking about also decreasing unemployment compensation. We are talking about reducing food stamps. If we are going to stimulate unemployment, we should be thinking about increases in unemployment compensation, increases in food stamps, income maintenance. Will you explain those?

REPRESENTATIVE GIAIMO: Those are reforms. The reduction in unemployment compensation is a reform in the formula. The reduction in food stamps is a reform in the food stamp formula. It is not designed to reduce assistance to unemployed people or to people who need food stamps.

It is a reform of some of the abuses that are presently in the system.

MR. HILL: Would the budget still be balanced if we had higher levels of unemployment, meaning that we were closer to a recession, and would we still be able to meet the expected increases in unemployment compensation?

SENATOR PROXMIRE: If we have a recession with increased unemployment, the budget will not be balanced no matter what. There is no question about it.

We must keep in mind, however, several things. Only about 25 percent of the budget goes for the poor or the near poor. Highway programs can be cut. Space programs can be cut. Public works programs can be cut. Fat can be cut from the military without hurting the poor. The poor are hurt more by inflation than almost any other group. They must pay more for the necessities of life. They must pay more for their housing. They must pay more for their food. They must pay more for all kinds of things that they have to have.

So it is perfectly consistent to have a program that is more just and more helpful to the people who need help in this country without feeling that the program is inconsistent or reactionary.

This is a program that helps if it helps low income people.

MR. DALY: Representative Giaimo, is there an increase in unemployment built into the projections on which the budget is based in concurrent budget resolution?

REPRESENTATIVE GIAIMO: Unemployment compensation is an entitlement program. It's one of the uncontrollables. It depends on our estimate of what the economy will be and what the unemployment rate will be. Whether it is high enough we do not know.

TED CORMANEY, staff of Senator William Roth (Republican, Delaware): What's wrong with putting a legal limit on federal spending? What's wrong with pegging federal spending to a percentage of gross national product? The number twenty-one comes to mind.

SENATOR PROXMIRE: Absolutely nothing. I voted for it. I am for it. I hope we can do it. The only question is whether or not it can be done in 1981. I voted for it in 1981. I thought Senator Edmund Muskie made a very powerful case, which was extremely difficult to do. He argued that we needed to cut $46 billion out of the budget, and he asked us to show him how to do that, and it was a pretty tough challenge for any of us to meet. But I think that the notion of having a 21 percent limit and then a 20 percent limit progressively is right. I think we should concentrate on that even more than on balancing the budget.

MR. CORMANEY: Maybe it is 21.37. What's wrong with a lid? What's wrong with a limit?

SENATOR PROXMIRE: Nothing, in my view.

REPRESENTATIVE GIAIMO: There is nothing wrong with a limit, and I have introduced a bill that includes a limit. I'm all for trying to bring in several other factors, one of which is tax expenditures. I think we have to have a lid on spending. I think we have to have a lid on tax expenditures, and I think we have to have a lid on loan guarantees and direct loans.

Part of the problem in Congress is that we do not have to do as the state legislatures do. Many state legislatures vote their spending, and then they have to have the revenue to meet it. For two centuries, Congress has merrily voted to set up programs, and then, if we didn't have the revenues to pay for those programs, we'd go out and borrow it. We've borrowed so much that we now have a debt of about $900 billion. There must be some discipline on us. It should not be a constitutional amendment; that is unnecessarily rigid. But there should be a discipline, such as a ceiling that is a certain percentage of GNP. If an emergency requires going beyond that, then the Congress would have to vote to do it. And that would be a discipline.

MR. DALY: Representative Reuss, would you like to speak on this one?

REPRESENTATIVE REUSS: I have no objection to this kind of chinning bar, and then let the public, in a democracy, vote whether they want more libraries or more private sector spending. That's the decision.

PAUL WONNECOTT, University of Maryland: Dr. Burns and Senator Proxmire talk about the tendency of taxes to rise as inflation pushes people up into higher and higher brackets. I would like to get their views on the indexation of the tax brackets. That is, do you think that tax brackets should automatically, by law, be increased in line with inflation so that inflation of itself does not push people up into higher tax brackets?

DR. BURNS: I oppose indexation because we don't have a strong enough constituency now fighting inflation. We would lose a good part of the constituency that we do have if we resorted to indexation. That's why I don't want it. I want to enlarge the constituency.

SENATOR PROXMIRE: Let me tell you why I favor it. I favor it for exactly the opposite reason. I think you'd have a much stronger constituency. Consider the situation now. We automatically have a tax increase every year that we have inflation. If we index taxes, that would mean that Congress would have to go on the line. Congressmen would have to admit to their constituents that they voted for a tax increase. That's a lot tougher than simply having inflation take care of it.

And we voted for what? With all the tax increases we've been talking about, revenue increases, we have had six income tax and other tax reductions by the Congress. We go home and we take bows for cutting taxes. That's baloney. We're not cutting taxes. What's happening is that inflation automatically increases taxes for us. And when we feel like it, in an election year, we cut those taxes a little. We get credit for a tax cut. So I'm for indexation.

DR. BURNS: All that I know is that countries that practice indexation find that their inflation rates stay up there and keep on rising.

SENATOR PROXMIRE: I agree with you that we should not have indexation anymore in other areas. We should do our best to resist indexation of wages, for example. But an exception should be made for taxes.

REPRESENTATIVE GIAIMO: I was recently in Israel, where they have indexation on just about everything. They have an inflation rate of about 100 percent. Their leaders told me to stay away from indexing; it's the ruination of a country.

REPRESENTATIVE REUSS: Indexation of taxes will turn a balanced budget into a deficit awfully fast. Think about that.

SENATOR PROXMIRE: It will tend to hold taxes down unless Congress steps in and increases them. One of the reasons we spend as much as we do is because the tax revenues have been rising. This should be the one exception. This is kind of inverted indexation. But I agree with you wholeheartedly on indexing income.

REPRESENTATIVE GIAIMO: The only reason that a lot of our colleagues in Congress will bite the bullet, if they will, and vote to cut spending is because they are fearful of the reactions back home. One of the ways in which that is reflected back home is that constituents are angry over the increased taxes they are paying, among other things.

SENATOR PROXMIRE: What really concerns them is if their representative increases their taxes by voting for higher taxes.

REPRESENTATIVE GIAIMO: They are sending a message to our colleagues to join us in reduction. And if we index taxes, we make it easier. Then they won't have that incentive to complain as much. That's what I'm afraid of.

STEVE ROBERTS, staff, Senate Banking Committee: We have two serious problems. One is low productivity and the other is low savings. How do we get both these rates to grow at something that's closer to our long-run historical potential?

REPRESENTATIVE REUSS: Congress did something very recently, for which Senator Proxmire and I can take modest credit. For years, the small saver has been badly discriminated against. He's been told that, while large savers can get 15 percent in the money market, he must be content with 5 or 5¼ percent at a bank or thrift institution. We have now done away with that nonsensical limitation. That will help some.

Again, of course, the best way to encourage savings is to get inflation down. Then there is something to save for.

DR. BURNS: The legislation recently passed by the Congress is excellent legislation, taken as a whole.

SENATOR PROXMIRE: You're talking about the Proxmire-Reuss Bill? [Laughter.]

DR. BURNS: I'm talking about the Proxmire-Reuss Bill, and both of you deserve great credit.

If I know the provisions of this act, the interest rate that can be paid by banks and thrift institutions on passbook savings can go up by one-fourth of 1 percent eighteen months from now. This is of some benefit. But we are proceeding at a snail's pace to help the little saver in the country.

REPRESENTATIVE REUSS: Correction, correction.

SENATOR PROXMIRE: It phases it out over a six-year period. It starts very slowly because we want the institutions to be able to adapt to that.

Furthermore, it allows interest on checking accounts for the first time. And, of course, that will encourage people to save through their checking accounts.

We are moving. Representative Reuss and I would both have preferred to move much more rapidly, but we had great resistance, understandably, from the institutions that complained about their increased costs.

REPRESENTATIVE REUSS: Dr. Burns, let me make you a happy man. The legislation, fortunately, does not do what you suggested. It does not say the interest rate can only go up at the rate of ¼ percent. The regulatory agencies may, and, indeed, are encouraged to, remove the ceiling entirely tomorrow. But if they do go slowly, we want at least some progress. There is, however, nothing to stop the regulatory agencies from taking off the limitation.

SENATOR PROXMIRE: In fact, the legislation positively encouraged the regulatory agencies to act a little more rapidly than they possibly can.

REPRESENTATIVE REUSS: Absolutely.

SENATOR PROXMIRE: Just as much as they can, consistent with the help of these institutions.

REPRESENTATIVE REUSS: Subject to that, I hope they'll take it off very soon.

SENATOR PROXMIRE: Let me answer Steve Roberts's questions. We encourage savings also, by establishing the principle in the windfall profits tax of exempting $200 of interest per person, or $400 for a couple, from the income tax. That encourages people to save money.

We need to work much harder than we have on productivity, because that is right at the heart of our inflation problem. Saving is one way of doing it. We probably have to have an even more generous investment credit. Other countries do have that.

REPRESENTATIVE REUSS: I'm going to quarrel a little bit with Senator Proxmire. I don't think that's such a great provision in the windfall profits tax. In fact, I voted against it. It allows a family that gets dividends from corporate stock to receive double the amount, $400 a year, in tax-free dividends. I love people who make their living by clipping coupons, but nothing at all was done for those who make their living by the sweat of their brows. I think it's most inequitable at a time when we're allegedly fighting inflation to unbalance the budget by $4½ billion by that provision.

SENATOR PROXMIRE: The overwhelming majority of those people have sweated plenty to save that money, and they paid taxes on it once when they sweated. We should force people to pay taxes on interest, but a very modest break for the small saver when saving is in such dire shape, it seems to me, is a wise decision.

DR. BURNS: I can agree with both of you. Here is a piece of legislation that will do so little for savings, and why should I disagree with what you say or with what my friend Henry Reuss says?

To encourage productivity in this country we need to reduce taxes that are paid by our business firms, and we need substantial and continued tax reductions: the kind of program that I suggested, legislation scheduling tax reductions over each of the next five to seven years, the reduction to become substantial in the third year, but only minor in the present year. Then, as far as the business world is concerned, businessmen would have a new environment in which to plan, to innovate, and to invest.

I also think that the capital gains tax, which Congress reduced in the Revenue Act of 1978—actually, that was good, constructive legislation—ought to be lowered further. I see no reason for retaining it. People are now paying capital gains taxes on phantom capital gains. It makes no sense at all if you want an environment in which productivity will be enhanced.

SENATOR PROXMIRE: I agree with that. I would, however, like to see us repeal the corporation income tax. The corporation income tax is a regressive tax in my view. It works out ultimately as a sales tax. It encourages featherbedding on the part of corporations. The corporations assume that Uncle Sam will get a great deal of their profits anyway, so there is no reason why they should not hire people they do not need.

The corporate income tax also prevents vigorous, profitable young enterprises—which could compete effectively, thereby helping to hold down prices—from growing as they should. If that income were simply taxed once when the stockholder received it and taxed at that level, the system would be more equitable. I'm delighted to see the *New York Times*, which is a very liberal paper, supporting that view.

REPRESENTATIVE REUSS: I see our tax system, like the enchanted cathedral, slowly sinking into the sea. [Laughter.]

REPRESENTATIVE GIAIMO: Another area we ought to look at in our efforts to increase productivity is the question of overregulation in government. We ought to look at our environmental laws. Part of the problem is that there is a pendulum effect in government, and the pendulum has swung altogether too far in one direction, putting American businessmen at a terrible disadvantage vis-à-vis foreign businesses and foreign competitors.

We must create a better climate, particularly in relation to foreign business and foreign competition. We are at a disadvantage in the world because of the infringements and the fetters that we put on industries, businessmen, and investors. I don't want to sound too pro-business, but the fact is that I am a Democrat, a liberal Democrat, and I recognize what we have done, what I have done these past twenty years. We must change that climate by bringing that pendulum back a little bit. Otherwise, we will be at a terrible competitive disadvantage, certainly with the Japanese and the Germans, among others.

BOB GOSS, National Conference of State Legislatures: Several of the panelists have intimated that, in order to combat inflation, they believe we should have a balanced budget or a budget in surplus not only for Fiscal Year 1981, but also for 1982, 1983, and following years. If we are successful in bringing on the impending recession in 1981, with its consequent increase in unemployment, is it still your position that we should have a balanced budget or budget in surplus in 1982 and 1983?

SENATOR PROXMIRE: I maintain that we cannot have a balanced budget in a recession year, no matter how hard we try. If we try, I think we will deepen the recession. But recessions are the exception. We have a recession normally maybe one or two years in ten. Every year we do not have a recession, we could definitely have a balanced budget. That should be our aim.

REPRESENTATIVE GIAIMO: There is one other factor, too, and that is if there is a recession, unemployment compensation goes up. No question about it. Probably, too, some specific targeted jobs programs will have to be increased to help alleviate the suffering.

That still leaves billions of dollars in other types of activities with which we literally are financing state and local budgets. They are dependent on the federal government. When I go home and talk to mayors in my district, they want to know what we are doing so they can put these programs into their budgets.

They are overly dependent on the federal government. We must move them away from that, and not just this year but for five or six years if we are ever to succeed in really bringing down the high inflation.

SENATOR PROXMIRE: Let me just quickly put that into perspective. The fact is that in the last eighteen years we have had one surplus, one. During most of that period, we have had very substantial growth. Growth in some years of 6 and 7 percent with a deficit. Ridiculous, disgraceful kind of an operation. In 1968 we had a deficit with about 3 percent unemployment. This call for a balanced budget in the years of prosperity and in normal years with normal growth represents a turnaround from what we have had in the past. It is perfectly consistent with saying that a deficit is probably inevitable in a recession year, which is a rare kind of situation.

DR. BURNS: I can endorse enthusiastically Senator Proxmire's statement, and I want to add a word about history. Go back to the recession of 1953–1954. During that recession government spending kept going down and going down rather sharply, but the objective of government at the time was to create an atmosphere of confidence among business people and among consumers. I was in the government at that time, and we developed policies to create confidence even in the face of declining government expenditures. This is a chapter of history worth recalling.

MARVIN KOSTERS, American Enterprise Institute: I would like to ask Congressman Reuss a question. He described for us a central fortress in his program that involves structural reforms for a rickety economy. I am wondering what sorts of things were meant in that regard. You mentioned a few things, such as sending a committee to Detroit to see what kinds of automobiles were being produced, requiring bankers to report on unworthy loans they might be making, and so on. I wonder what other elements there might be in the program.

REPRESENTATIVE REUSS: I would take a leaf from the books of the Germans and the Japanese, who have both achieved economic miracles. One of the ways they have achieved that is through government-business-labor teams that, instead of confrontation, try cooperation.

Five years ago the Japanese saw their leading industry, textiles, about to fold because there were plenty of looms and spindles in Korea, Taiwan, and Singapore that were stealing Japan's textile business. Instead of building protectionist barriers or running around in circles and seeing vast unemployment and a ruined textile industry, the Japanese team put their minds on it, bringing together capital and labor regulations and spectral planning, and put into place a whole new industry, consumer electronics. So today, when a Japanese worker in an obsolete textile factory loses his job because the factory closes, he goes across the street to an up-and-coming electronics plant and gets a better job there.

That's called planning. I know planning is in disrepute, but every business in this country that is successful uses it. I cannot for the life of me see why we can't put a little thought and elbow-grease into this and do some planning ourselves so that we don't have fiascos like our automobile situation, our steel problem, our railroad collapse. That's what I mean. We haven't tried it. I'd like to see us try it.

SENATOR PROXMIRE: To a very considerable extent, that could be done consistent with holding down spending. In fact, it would encourage the private sector to do a bigger job. It's not a program of more government intervention in the sense that we would have to spend more money or tax more. It's a program of encouraging industry to move forward. Dr. Burns suggested to our committee years ago that we should have productivity councils that should work along somewhat similar lines to improve productivity.

REPRESENTATIVE REUSS: Absolutely. That's the whole thing, and it doesn't cost anything except a little brain work.

DR. BURNS: The kind of planning I would like to see in particular is planning for a sense of stability in governmental policy itself, and that is what we lack at the present time. An American businessman doesn't know what may happen tomorrow. He's lost all sense of continuity and stability in financial policy. To adhere to a sound financial plan has become essential to our future.

REPRESENTATIVE REUSS: It is this method of stop-start-stop-go, green light, red light that drives everybody up a wall, and it has brought us, I won't say to our knees, but to a position where I don't like to see us.

MR. ROBERTS: To build a better sense of stability, would it be advantageous to have multi-year budgeting and multi-year targets for monetary policy?

REPRESENTATIVE GIAIMO: It probably would. We are trying to work toward that goal, as you know. The President is trying to do it, and we in the Congress are trying to adopt multi-year budgeting.

The difficulty, however, is that we have enough trouble foreseeing—and the economists have been wrong for several years—what will happen in 1981, let alone in 1982 and 1983. So all I'm saying is that, while it's good to try to have multi-year budgeting, we must recognize that there may be big swings in the later years.

DR. BURNS: I think it is also an abstract question. It all depends on the quality of multi-year budgeting. Take, for example, the President's January budget message. That budget message presented budget projections on government spending and governmental revenues into 1984 and 1985. Look at the figure on federal spending even for the Fiscal Year 1984 that is presented in this January's budget message. If we compare that figure with the figure for fiscal 1984 that was presented a year ago, we find that it is higher by $165 billion. That kind of multi-year budgeting only causes confusion, even dismay and consternation in business circles on which we have to depend, if the rest of us are to be able to live the way we think we should.

I favor multi-year budgeting, but I favor multi-year budgeting of much higher quality than the kind we have recently experienced.

SENATOR PROXMIRE: In addition to the difficulty with quality, congressmen are elected every two years, the president every four years, and senators every six years. We cannot bind a future Congress. A new Congress will be elected in 1982, a new president will be elected this year. They will do exactly what they want to do. They may disagree entirely with what we plan. Multi-year budgeting is difficult, but we should try to influence the future Congresses in every way we can.

It is much more practical to have multi-year targets for the Federal Reserve. Federal Reserve members are appointed for fourteen years. They can operate on a more stable basis; they are insulated, to a very considerable degree, from politics. They can follow a multi-year program of gradually reducing the rate of increase in the money supply as one way of combating inflation.

REPRESENTATIVE REUSS: The monetary question does lend itself to multi-year projections. The Federal Reserve would do well in the years to come to keep a slow and steady growth of the money supply consistent with the increase in productivity that we ought to be getting back to, and not panic at every sign of too much activity or too little activity.

I would like to hear Dr. Burns's current thought on that.

Dr. Burns: We have had an explosion of financial technology in our country. If we look at the narrowly defined money supply that the Federal Reserve has adhered to for a long time, and which people in government and in business follow so closely, we find that between September 1978 and March 1979 the money supply declined.

If we take a more comprehensive measure of the money supply, one that I follow particularly since I left the Federal Reserve, it showed an actual increase of 10 percent as an annual rate. Multi-year targeting of the money supply, therefore, in an era when financial technology is exploding, is very hard. It is easy enough to budget for it, but to adhere to it when financial technology is changing would be unwise. We must adapt, in part, to the world of finance, which is changing around us very rapidly.

Representative Giaimo: That is why, Dr. Burns, it is so hard to get quality in those projections, because of the great role played by inflation and these other imponderables that you're talking about.

Mr. Daly: As I said earlier, monetary policy is a very sophisticated subject.

This concludes another public policy forum presented by the American Enterprise Institute for Public Policy Research. On behalf of AEI, our hearty thanks to the distinguished and expert panelists: Senator Proxmire, Dr. Burns, Representative Giaimo, and Representative Reuss. Our thanks also to our guests and experts attending the forum for their participation.